Meet Ruben and R[...]
Today they go to P[lay Zone Park].
They like the rides and games.

Ruben likes to play a ball game.
He aims for the tire tube.
"I made a goal!" he yells.

Rosa plays the beanbag game.
She throws five beanbags in a boat.
"I made it!" she screams.

Ruben and Rosa see a fast ride go by.
It is the Fire Racer!

The Fire Racer climbs and dives.
It makes huge turns.
It leans from side to side.

Ruben and Rosa cannot wait to ride.
They take a seat on Fire Racer.
They wave as the ride begins.

"Here we go!" they say.
Fire Racer seems to fly.
Ruben and Rosa smile and scream.

"That ride is the best!
May we go one more time?" asks Ruben.